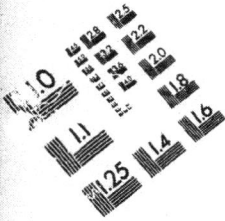

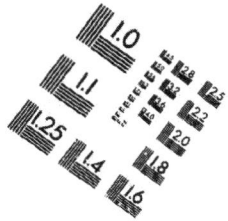

IMAGE EVALUATION
TEST TARGET (MT-3)

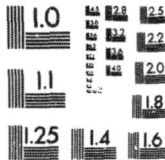

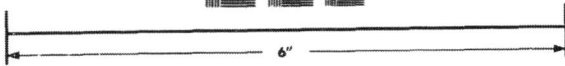

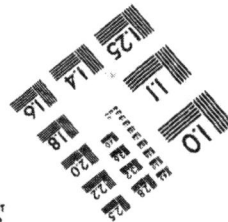

6"

Photographic
Sciences
Corporation

23 WEST MAIN STREET
WEBSTER, N.Y. 14580
(716) 872-4503

CIHM/ICMH
Microfiche
Series.

CIHM/ICMH
Collection de
microfiches.

Canadian Institute for Historical Microreproductions / Institut canadien de microreproductions historiques

© 1985

Technical and Bibliographic Notes/Notes techniques et bibliographiques

The Institute has attempted to obtain the best
original copy available for filming. Features of this
copy which may be bibliographically unique,
which may alter any of the images in the
reproduction, or which may significantly change
the usual method of filming, are checked below.

☐ Coloured covers/
Couverture de couleur

☐ Covers damaged/
Couverture endommagée

☐ Covers restored and/or laminated/
Couverture restaurée et/ou pelliculée

☐ Cover title missing/
Le titre de couverture manque

☐ Coloured maps/
Cartes géographiques en couleur

☐ Coloured ink (i.e. other than blue or black)/
Encre de couleur (i.e. autre que bleue ou noire)

☐ Coloured plates and/or illustrations/
Planches et/ou illustrations en couleur

☐ Bound with other material/
Relié avec d'autres documents

☐ Tight binding may cause shadows or distortion
along interior margin/
La reliure serrée peut causer de l'ombre ou de la
distortion le long de la marge intérieure

☐ Blank leaves added during restoration may
appear within the text. Whenever possible, these
have been omitted from filming/
Il se peut que certaines pages blanches ajoutées
lors d'une restauration apparaissent dans le texte,
mais, lorsque cela était possible, ces pages n'ont
pas été filmées.

☐ Additional comments:/
Commentaires supplémentaires:

L'Institut a microfilmé le meilleur exemplaire
qu'il lui a été possible de se procurer. Les détails
de cet exemplaire qui sont peut-être uniques du
point de vue bibliographique, qui peuvent modifier
une image reproduite, ou qui peuvent exiger une
modification dans la méthode normale de filmage
sont indiqués ci-dessous.

☐ Coloured pages/
Pages de couleur

☐ Pages damaged/
Pages endommagées

☐ Pages restored and/or laminated/
Pages restaurées et/ou pelliculées

☑ Pages discoloured, stained or foxed/
Pages décolorées, tachetées ou piquées

☐ Pages detached/
Pages détachées

☑ Showthrough/
Transparence

☐ Quality of print varies/
Qualité inégale de l'impression

☐ Includes supplementary material/
Comprend du matériel supplémentaire

☐ Only edition available/
Seule édition disponible

☐ Pages wholly or partially obscured by errata
slips, tissues, etc., have been refilmed to
ensure the best possible image/
Les pages totalement ou partiellement
obscurcies par un feuillet d'errata, une pelure,
etc., ont été filmées à nouveau de façon à
obtenir la meilleure image possible.

This item is filmed at the reduction ratio checked below/
Ce document est filmé au taux de réduction indiqué ci-dessous.

10X		14X		18X		22X		26X		30X	
						✓					
	12X		16X		20X		24X		28X		32X

MILITARY MEMOIR

OF THE LATE

LIEUTENANT-GENERAL

SIR JOHN MACLEOD, G.C.H.

SENIOR COLONEL COMMANDANT

AND

DIRECTOR GENERAL OF ARTILLERY.

JANUARY, 1834.

LONDON:

Printed for R. and C. BYFIELD,
21, Charing Cross.

MILITARY MEMOIR

SIR JOHN MACLEOD, G.C.H.

MANY of Sir John Macleod's friends
have expressed an earnest wish of
possessing some document of his military career; and the desire of complying with their wishes has led to a
compilation from his papers, which
forms the subject of the following
Memoir.   Their wishes ought, perhaps, to have been sooner attended
to : but to undertake a retrospective
view of so long a service is in itself
an attempt of no common difficulty;

and it will be well understood, that private feelings have shrunk from a task, which it is felt no effort can do justice to.

The friends of Sir John Macleod are aware, that the nature of his public services does not afford extensive subject for narrative. He was the spring of action in others, more than a partaker in events that prospered chiefly from his judgment: his was the anxious charge of responsibility; of foresight and superintending control, more than of active participation in what emanated from him: and his services are better recorded in the successes and rewards of others, and in the high name and public estimation of his corps, than in details relating merely personally to himself.

His earliest services commenced in command; and are those which partake most of active character. These occurred at a period of momentous interest to his country; and drawing public notice and distinction on him, even at that early period of his life, afforded a sure and unerring earnest of those superior qualities that marked his subsequent career.

Sir John Macleod joined the Royal Military Academy at Woolwich as a cadet, in the year 1767; and obtained a commission, as Second Lieutenant, on the 15th of March, 1771.

On obtaining his commission he was

ordered to Gibraltar, where he had an opportunity, on a large scale, of viewing and practising the garrison duties of his profession.

In 1774 he returned to England, and solicited leave of absence, with a view of making an extended professional tour on the continent. He settled, in the first instance, at the college of St. Omer, and was still engaged in general studies there, when, in the following year, he was recalled to England, in order to join the forces preparing to suppress the colonial rebellion in North America. He arrived at Portsmouth at the end of the year; the expedition was then daily expected to proceed on its course, assembling previous to its final departure at Cork.

Little occurred on his first arrival in America, beyond the usual events of ordinary service. His letters are dated, in 1776, from South Carolina; from Philadelphia in 1777-8; from Rhode Island in 1779; and from Charles Town in 1780.

In 1781, he joined the force detached under Earl Cornwallis, which he accompanied into North Carolina, during an arduous march of above six hundred miles; and he had the good fortune to command the artillery, engaged in the signal victory of Guilford, over the combined continental and American forces, on the 15th of March.

8

In describing his movements previous
to the battle, Lord Cornwallis ob-
serves: " The woods on the right
" and left were reported to be im-
" practicable for cannon ; but as that
" on our right appeared to be most
" open, I resolved to attack the left
" wing of the enemy ; and whilst my
" disposition was making for that pur-
" pose, I ordered Lieutenant Macleod
" to bring forward the guns and can-
" nonade their centre."

Again, the dispatch describing a
critical period of the battle states, the
second battalion of guards having
defeated a corps of continental infantry, much superior in number, formed
on the open field, and captured two six-

pounders ; but pursuing with too much ardour, they became exposed to an attack from Washington's dragoons, with the loss of the six-pounders they had taken : it then mentions that the enemy's cavalry were soon repulsed, by a well-directed fire from the guns just brought up by Lieutenant Macleod ; and on the appearance of the grenadiers of the guards, and the 71st regiment, the guns were soon recaptured.

The exertions of the artillery under Sir John Macleod's orders on this service, in overcoming the obstacles opposed to their advance by the difficulties of the country, will be best appreciated by Lord Cornwallis's de-

scription of the march of the army previous to the battle of Guilford :—
" Their invincible patience, in the
" hardships and fatigues of a march
" of above six hundred miles, in which
" they have forded several large rivers
" and numberless creeks, many of
" which would be reckoned large rivers
" in any other country in the world,
" without tents, and often without
" provisions, will sufficiently manifest
" their ardent zeal for the honour and
" interests of their Sovereign and
" their Country."

During the course of this service Sir John Macleod had attained the rank of First Lieutenant (in July, 1779). His last letters from America are dated in 1781, just previous to his embarkation at New York to return to Europe, in the November of that year.

In January, 1782, he was promoted to the ɪank of Second Captain.

On the return of the army to England, Lord Cornwallis, wishing to mark in a distinguished manner his sense of Sir John Macleod's services while under his orders, more particularly in the battle of Guilford, and in the professional resources he had shown in the difficulties attending the previous march of the army, named him to the King; and his Majesty was pleased, in consequence, to command his personal attendance and presentation by Lord Cornwallis.

In the same year he was appointed
to the Staff of Lord George Lennox.

The regiment of artillery had been
increased, during the American war,
to four battalions and an invalid battalion ; and the Master General of
the Ordnance, from so great an aug-
mentation, found it necessary to ex-
tend its staff, at the head of which he
placed Sir John Macleod.

In 1790, Lord Cornwallis was appointed Governor General and Commander in Chief in India; and his
Lordship immediately expressed a desire that Sir John Macleod should
accompany him ; but his staff duties,
already forming an integral part of
the important discipline he was perfecting, compelled him to forego the

gratification of attending his commander and friend.

On the 14th of May, 1790, he succeeded to a company in the regiment of artillery.

We now approach a period, when the peculiar power and energies of Sir John Macleod's character were to be more conspicuously developed and brought into public notice. The war occasioned by the French Revolution worked rapid changes and improvements in the French army, which it became necessary to meet with corresponding efforts on our part. They had started and matured a system of warfare, and celerity of movement, peculiarly their own; and the other

nations of Europe soon learnt the
necessity of opposing them on their
own system. Their artillery, particularly, had undergone material change
and facility of movement; with our-
selves, similar changes were of course
studied and adopted. All field artillery was in future to have accelerated
activity of movement, beyond that of
infantry; and a portion of it was
trained to rival the movements of
cavalry. The first formation of horse
artillery, in the British army, was in
the early part of 1793. Two troops
were formed in January that year:
others were added in quick succession.
The organization and equipment of
this new arm, with the entire change

that followed in the whole nature and system of our field artillery, gave ample scope to the indefatigable mind of Sir John Macleod; and his unremitting attention and exertions were most ably met by the zeal and emulation of the officers appointed to the new commands.

At this time, there occurred another gratifying instance of the high estimation in which Sir John Macleod's name was held in the army.

An expedition was preparing under the command of the late Marquess of Hastings, with whom he had served in America. His first step, in preparing his arrangements, was to offer the command of the artillery to Sir John

Macleod; but not only did his staff duties again present an impediment, but his rank in the service at the time precluded the possibility of his appointment to so large a command.ª

The regiment of artillery had now been augmented from the peace establishment, to a force of 25,000 men. The staff duties had of course increased in proportion, both in trust, and in importance. The Master-General in consequence, in concurrence with the Duke of York, Commander-in-Chief, submitted a representation to His Majesty, of the indispensable necessity of a public officer as Deputy Adjutant General of Artillery. His

ª See Appendix (A.)

Majesty was pleased to approve of this arrangement; and Sir John Macleod was accordingly appointed Deputy Adjutant-General, with the rank of Lieutenant-Colonel in the army. (March 27th, 1795).

On the 21st August, 1797, he was promoted to the regimental rank of Lieutenant-Colonel.

In 1798, a rebellion of most disastrous character broke forth in Ireland; and Lord Cornwallis was called on to proceed thither, with extended authority to suppress it by force of arms, Sir John Macleod considered the active employment of the Master-General of the Ordnance a favourable moment for soliciting permission to

accompany him ; and he entreated
Lord Cornwallis to submit his wishes
to the King, and to exert his influence
with His Majesty, to that effect. He
received on this occasion a most kind
and gracious assurance of the King's
approval of his zeal and motives ; but
his absence from his responsible duties
was considered inadmissible.[b]

In addition to the increased extent
of the corps, there was added, in 1801,
the establishment of a riding school,
on a large and efficient scale ; and
also a veterinary establishment adequate to the necessities of the cavalry
branches of the regiment ; now increased by a numerous corps of drivers,
regularly organized and trained for

the service of field brigades of artillery. This corps, which had its first formation in 1793, had grown to the extent of 5500 officers and men; and before the conclusion of the war, amounted to 7300. The formation and efficiency of these several departments, though apparently of minor detail and interest in the service, were not the less an object of Sir John Macleod's constant care and watchful superintendence.

In 1808, Sir John Macleod was directed to organize a tenth battalion of artillery.

On the death of Lieutenant-General Walton, in the same year, he was appointed to succeed that officer as Master Gunner of England.

In 1809, the Scheldt expedition was projected; and Lord Chatham being at the time Master-General of the Ordnance, Sir John Macleod again seized the opportunity for soliciting active employment. His Majesty on this occasion was pleased to accede to his request; and he accordingly sailed from the Downs in command of the artillery under Lord Chatham's orders, in July, 1809.

The result of this expedition is remembered to have been unsuccessful; but the arduous and laborious duties of Sir John Macleod's command proceeded from the commencement of the operations with uninterrupted and progressive success; doing equal honour

to the arrangements of the commanding officer, and the devoted zeal of
the corps, in surmounting every ob-
stacle, as far as the objects of the expedition were persevered in.   On the
final abandonment of its ulterior views,
Sir John Macleod returned to England[c].

At no previous period had the resources of Sir John Macleod's mind
been more necessarily exerted, than
in the gigantic outfit of this expedition.   But the war now assumed a
character that called for still increasing energy and thought to meet
the demands and casualties of the
service, multiplied by the extension of
our arms throughout every part of

the world, by a constantly accumu-
lating correspondence from every
quarter, and above all, the hourly
increasing importance of the war in
the Peninsula, where the vigour of
the struggle between the two con-
tending nations seemed actually to
grow with its duration. Sir John
Macleod fortunately possessed, and
knew how to employ, a mind devoted
to the most arduous undertakings of
the service; and the growing emer-
gencies of such an important moment
to the country, continued to give new
life to his ardent and energetic exertions.

Before the close of the war, the
three corps of artillery organized by

Sir John Macleod amounted to up-
wards of 26,000 men, and near 14,000
horses. The recruiting branch of the
service alone, to keep up such " a
legion" in men and horses, had be-
come a source of great and anxious
solicitude ; and formed in itself an
overpowering mass of business, to any
mind of less resource or experience
than his own. From the commencement of the revolutionary war, also,
there had been an almost constant
succession of foreign expeditions, the
arrangement and equipment of which
devolved upon him. The principal
of these were the Continental in 1793,
the West Indies in 1794, the Cape of
Good Hope in 1795, the Helder in

1799, Egypt in 1800, Cape of Good
Hope in 1806, Buenos Ayres in 1807,
the Mediterranean throughout the
war, Spain and Portugal in 1808, Walcheren in 1809, Holland in 1813, and
finally, the Netherlands and France
in 1815.

On the 25th October, 1809, he attained the rank of Major-General;
and on the 4th June, 1814, the rank
of Lieutenant-General in the army.

In 1820, his late Majesty, desirous
of marking his sense of Sir John Macleod's long and important services,
commanded his attendance at the
Pavilion at Brighton, where, under
circumstances of peculiar kindness
and distinction, he conferred on him

the honour of Knighthood, and appointed him Grand Cross of the Royal Guelphic Order[d].

The Battle of Waterloo at length gave peace to Europe; and on the recall of the British army of occupation from France, Sir John Macleod was employed in making similar reductions in the artillery, to those which took place in all branches of the service. He had now attained a rank which, from the reduced numbers of the corps, would in future prevent his employment in the duties he had fulfilled during the war. It was on this occasion he received a letter from the Duke of Wellington, offering him the situation of Director-General of

Artillery. A mind like Sir John Macleod's could not with indifference quit a post at which he may be said to have formed the corps, to whose name and welfare he was, in every sense and feeling, enthusiastically devoted : and the considerate kindness with which the Duke's proposal was addressed to him, was never forgotten by him. He continued to fulfil the duties of Director-General of Artillery to the close of his life; and even throughout his last illness, he would never consent to any respite from the details and duties of his trust.

If we revert to the services of Sir John Macleod throughout the eventful and protracted war, during which he was employed in the most confidential and important duties an officer can fulfil, it would be difficult to distinguish what might properly be termed the most conspicuous period of his career: but it may perhaps be considered to be that between the interval commencing with the chivalrous and enterprising advance of Sir John Moore into Spain, and the brilliant succession of events that followed without intermission, till the final close of operations in the Peninsula; at which time the nature and responsibility of the duties he controlled had acquired an extent, variety, and importance, quite unequalled in our service.

Sir John Macleod was married, in

the year 1783, to Lady Amelia Kerr,
second daughter of the fourth Marquess of Lothian, and had a family
of four sons and five daughters.

It may be permitted here briefly
to advert, with his own, to services
which were fostered by him, and
which bore no common character in
the army.

Lieutenant-Colonel Charles Macleod, who fell while leading the 43rd
regiment in the storming of Badajoz,
in 1812, had, from the period of his
first entering the army, given proof
of his ardent attachment to the service,
and a promise of the fame and rare
distinction that recorded the close of
his brilliant career.

His services commenced under his
father's friend, Lord Cornwallis; he
was with him in India when he died,
and was the bearer of the despatches
to England announcing that melan-
choly event. He was next employed
at Copenhagen, and subsequently in
the Peninsula. His character and
services are best recorded in the
words of the illustrious Commander,
who, with the glory of his own deeds,
has transmitted the name of Colonel
Macleod to posterity. The following
is an extract from the Duke of Wellington's despatch announcing the fall
of Badajoz in 1812.

" In Lieutenant-Colonel Macleod,
" of the 43rd regiment, who was killed

" in the breach, his Majesty has sus-
" tained the loss of an officer who
" was an ornament to his profession,
" and was capable of rendering the
" most important services to his
" country."

Every soldier will understand, that
if anything could have afforded con-
solation to Sir John Macleod, on the
loss of such a son, it would have been
a tribute of this nature from such a
source. Even under the weight of
such a blow it had its influence:
the patriot father bowed in submis-
sion to his heavy affliction, and
buried his private griefs for ever in
his own breast*.

Sir John Macleod's second son commenced his service in the navy, under the late Lord Hugh Seymour; and afterwards obtained a commission in the Engineers. He was a most zealous officer, and distinguished himself at the siege of Scylla Castle; at the siege of Ciudad Roderigo; and at that of Badajoz, where he unfortunately received a wound from which he has never ceased to suffer.

His third son, James, was, in the first instance, in the Artillery, and employed at Copenhagen, at Walcheren, and throughout a great part of the Peninsular campaigns. In 1823 he quitted the Artillery and joined the 41st regiment, and was employed in the active operations

9

carrying on in India, when he fell a victim to the climate at Rangoon, in 1824.

Sir John Macleod's fourth son commenced his services likewise in the Artillery, and served in that corps in the battle of Talavera, and the early campaigns of the Peninsular war. On the death of Colonel Charles Macleod, the Duke of York offered him a commission in the Line; and it was while he was serving at the siege of Dantzic, where he had been sent on a special duty, that he was recalled in order to join the 35th regiment, then with the force under Lord Lynedoch's command, in Holland. He was next employed on the staff of the Duke of

Wellington's army in the Netherlands, and was severely wounded at Quatre-Bras, in the enemy's attack of the 16th of June. He proceeded subsequently to Canada, on the personal staff of the late Duke of Richmond; and, like his elder brother, it was his misfortune to have to bear to England the despatches announcing his friend and patron's death. He is at present on the staff of the army in Jamaica, where he has been employed since 1825.

From the general outline that has been given of Sir John Macleod's services, some faint impression may be formed of his character, by those who did not know him. The period at

which he served, was that of most
importance in his country's annals;
and his was a mind not to bear an
undistinguished part in the records of
the time. An unprecedented war, in
power and duration, had opened a
field for the development and full
exertion of its superior and peculiar
qualities. The leading feature of his
character was the confidence he in-
spired in others, and the unbounded
trust they reposed in him; and thus,
whether called on for counsel, or to
act under unforeseen or sudden emer-
gencies of service, he was ever ready
and prepared to meet its exigencies.
His watchfulness seemed never to
sleep, but to be in anticipation of

what might occur; and to forestal
events, by securing means to meet
them. " His whole soul," to use a
common-place expression, was in his
profession. Of every soldier he made
himself the friend. To his equals in
rank he was a brother; to those be-
neath him a father, in kindness and
in counsel; and to the private soldiers
a benefactor; ever watching over
their comfort and their welfare. To
all he had a ready ear to listen, and
a heart and hand to act in their be-
half. Throughout his long career he
was never known to act with the
slightest approach to severity; and
yet he never failed to maintain discipline, to reprove fault, or to check

irregularity. He animated zeal, ex-
cited energy, and aimed at perfecting
discipline, by always appealing to the
better and nobler feelings that prevail
with the soldier's character. His
influence extended beyond the branch
of the service he controlled ; his name
was a passport everywhere ; and held
in such universal respect, that it im-
posed emulation of good deeds on all
who belonged to him ; and the con-
duct and acts of his sons, however
they might reflect on him, were thought
of but as a matter of course in them :
even at the period of his son's fall at
Badajoz, his loss, as the *son*, was
almost as universally felt as in that of
the brilliant officer commanding a dis-

tinguished corps. Sir John Macleod's highest praises, however, are those which cannot be told the world : nor, indeed, is private character the proper subject of a memoir of this nature. Our private character, too, is always best judged and known by that of our associates and friends ; his were among the great and the good. Honoured by his Sovereign, respected by all ranks of the army, loved by his friends, and revered by his family, his private life afforded an example to all who love goodness, honour, and benevolence : while his professional career ever pointed to the highest and noblest attainments by which we can serve our country.

Sir John Macleod was of the Raaza family; and his grandfather, Colonel Eneas Macleod, served with great distinction in the campaigns and sieges of the Duke of Marlborough [f].

He was born the 29th of January, 1752, and died, the Father of his Corps, in the 82nd year of his age.

APPENDIX.

THE following letter is here given, not so much with a view of exemplifying the estimation in which the Marquess of Hastings held Sir John Macleod's services, as the desire which naturally suggests itself, of recording a proof so illustrative of the zeal and enterprise of his Lordship's character :

St. James's Place,
November 5th, 1793.

(Secret.)

MY DEAR MACLEOD,

It is probable that I may very

speedily be employed at the head of a con-
siderable force. In such a situation, there
is not any person I could so much wish for
a commander of my artillery, as yourself.
If this cannot be, point out to me somebody
upon whom I can rely in such a trust. Let
it be so been fellow, who will laugh in
the midst of difficulties, as I have seen you
do. Cast your eyes round, too, for inferior
officers whom I may ask for: because, as
we are sure of tough work, I ought to have
good stuff. Thirty pieces of cannon would
properly be requisite; yet I foresee, that
from the paucity of artillerymen, I shall be
stinted in this particular. I mention this,
to give you an idea what the nature of the
artillery officer's command would be. But
all is still loose and undetermined; and I

have to request your secrecy in every respect.

Believe me, &c.,

MOIRA.

(B.)

Whitehall, June 18*th,* 1798.

DEAR MACLEOD,

I am just returned from the King's closet, and have stated to him your earnest wish to be allowed to accompany me to Ireland, for a certain time at least, and the desire which I felt of availing myself of your services. His Majesty expressed himself to be highly pleased with your zealous offer; and to be much disposed to gratify both you and me, by complying with your request; but he added, that he was apprehensive that the service here must greatly suffer by the absence of the public officer; and he desired me to tell him fairly, whether that would not be the case.

Called upon in this manner for my opinion, I could not help admitting that the service here must be liable to some inconvenience from your absence; upon which his Majesty desired me, not to press him further on the subject.

I am sincerely sorry for this disappointment, on your account as well as my own; but on reflecting coolly on the business, I must confess I think the King is in the right.

Dear Macleod,

Very sincerely yours,

CORNWALLIS.

(C.)

It is scarcely possible to convey an adequate idea of the anxious and responsible

duties of a commanding officer of Artillery
on a service of this extended scale; more
particularly under circumstances where con-
tingencies are uncontrollable, and liable to
baffle or interfere with the best arrangements. The details of this expedition, however, have been so fully and frequently
before the world, in every form, that it has
not been considered necessary to insert here
any part of Sir John Macleod's Journal of
its operations.

(D.)

44, Grosvenor Place,
October 13th, 1820.

SIR,

It gives me great pleasure to have
to acquaint you, that his Majesty, in con-
sideration of your distinguished services,
and more particularly of the very able assist-

ance you gave on the forming the Artillery
attached to the King's German Legion, and
the zealous and judicious activity by which,
through a series of years, you contributed
so much to the flourishing state of that
gallant corps, has been most graciously
pleased to nominate and appoint you, Sir, a
Knight Grand Cross of the Royal Guelphic
Order, the decoration of which I have the
honour of transmitting to you herewith, and
remain, with the highest esteem,

Sir,

Your most obedient,

and very humble Servant,

MUNSTER.

*To Lieutenant General Sir John
Macleod, G.C.H., &c. &c.*

(E.)

The Officers of the 43rd Regiment, desirous of recording their affection and respect to their lamented Commander, erected a monument to his memory in Westminster Abbey, under the immediate superintendence of his friend, Colonel William Napier; on which is engraved the extract given from the Duke of Wellington's despatch.

(F.)

See Biggs's Military Chronicles.

LONDON·
Printed for R. and C. Byfield,
21, Charing Cross.

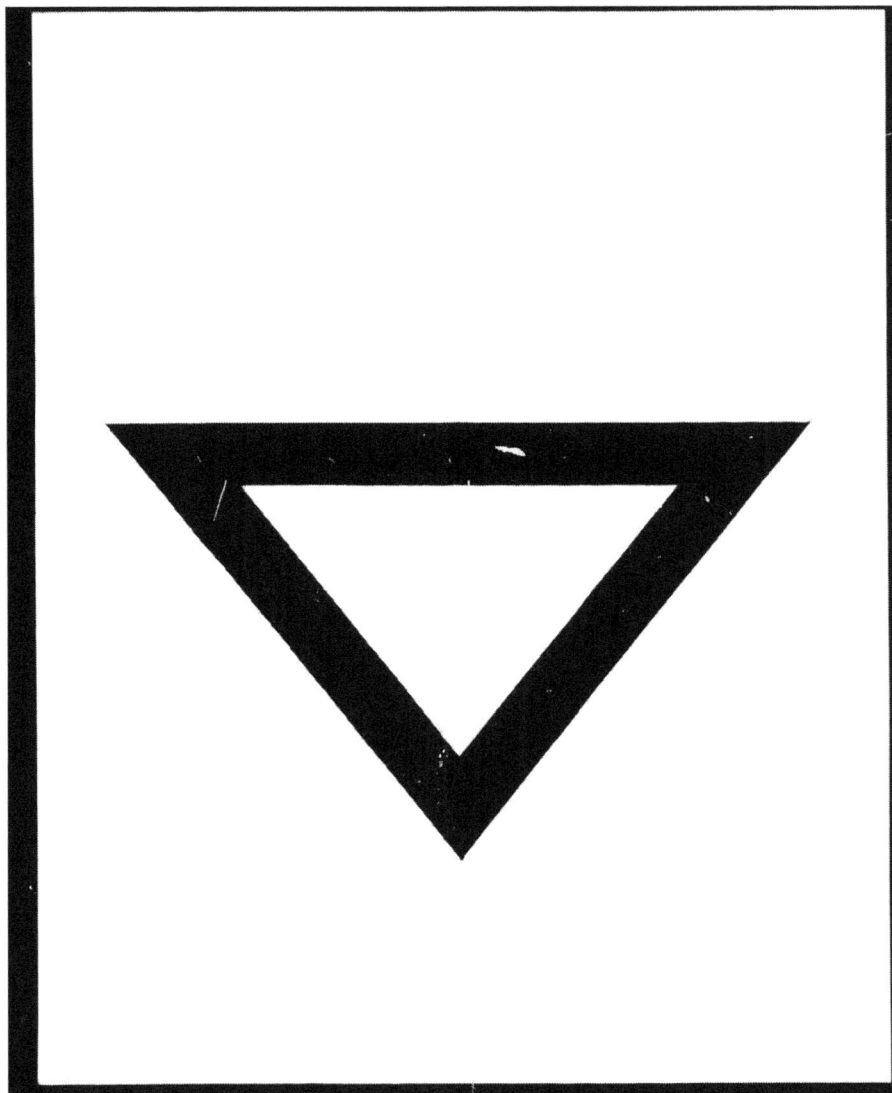

CPSIA information can be obtained
at www.ICGtesting.com
Printed in the USA
BVHW040000010222
627651BV00010B/634

9 781014 547941